THE
UK TAXATION
OF
MODERN FINANCIAL
INSTRUMENTS
& TRANSACTIONS

— • —

Derek A. Ross

PARTNER IN CHARGE OF INTERNATIONAL
TREASURY SERVICES, TOUCHE ROSS

CASSELL

First published 1989 by **Cassell Educational Ltd**
Artillery House, Artillery Row, London SW1P 1RT

Copyright © 1989 Touche Ross & Co.

British Library Cataloguing in Publication Data
Ross, Derek A.
   The UK taxation of modern financial instruments and
   transactions
   1. Great Britain. Companies. Financial transactions.
   Taxation. Law
   I. Title
   344.1036'7

ISBN 0-304-31831-0

Typeset by Activity Ltd., Salisbury, Wilts
Printed and bound in Great Britain by Biddles Ltd, Guildford and Kings Lynn

CONTENTS

Preface   v

The Author   vi

1   INTRODUCTION   1

2   GENERAL FEATURES OF THE UK TAX SYSTEM   2

2.1   Background   2
2.2   Groups   2
2.3   Capital and Revenue   3
2.4   Tax Status of Companies   3
2.5   Interest   4

3   FOREIGN EXCHANGE GAINS AND LOSSES   5

3.1   Introduction   5
3.2   *Pattison* v. *Marine Midland Ltd*   6
3.3   The Revenue's Reaction   7
3.4   Accountancy Practice   8
3.5   Statement of Practice SP1/87   9
3.6   Unmatched Positions   10
3.7   Currency Swaps   11
3.8   Hedging Transactions   12
3.9   Overseas Branches and Trades   12
3.10   Realisation Basis   13
3.11   Roundabouts   13
3.12   Non-trading Companies   14
3.13   Capital Allowances   15
3.14   Capital Gains   16

4   CURRENCY AND OTHER OPTIONS   19

4.1   Background   19
4.2   Basis of Taxation – Trading Transactions   20
4.3   Basis of Taxation – Non-trading Transactions   21
4.4   Recent Developments in Over-the-counter
Options   23

5	CURRENCY SWAPS	25
5.1	Explanation of Transaction	25
5.2	Tax Implications	27

6	LOAN FINANCE – MAIN TAX ISSUES	30
6.1	Interest Deductibility	30
6.2	Incidental Costs of Obtaining Loan Finance	32
6.3	Annual Payments	33
6.4	Investment and Other Non-trading Companies	34

7	QUOTED EUROBONDS	35

8	DEEP DISCOUNT SECURITIES	37
8.1	Definition	37
8.2	Basis of Taxation	37
8.3	TA 1988 Schedule 4	38
8.4	Coupon Stripping	40
8.5	Financial Traders	41

9	STERLING COMMERCIAL PAPER	42
9.1	Definition	42
9.2	Basis of Taxation	42

10	FINANCIAL FUTURES	45
10.1	Background	45
10.2	Basis of Taxation – Trading Transactions	45
10.3	Basis of Taxation – Non-trading Transactions	46
10.4	Statement of Practice SP4/88	47

11	INTEREST RATE SWAPS	48
11.1	Analysis of Transaction	48
11.2	Treatment of Compensatory Payments	49
11.3	Fees	51

12	FORWARD RATE AGREEMENTS (FRAs)	53
12.1	Background	53
12.2	Basis of Taxation	54

13	INTEREST RATE GUARANTEES (IRGs)	55
13.1	Background	55
13.2	Basis of Taxation	55

	Index	57

PREFACE

In order to be of the widest possible use, this book has been written in general terms. It is intended as a guide only, and its application to specific situations will depend upon the particular circumstances involved. Accordingly, it is recommended that the reader seek professional advice regarding any problems that he or she encounters, and this book should not be relied upon as a substitute for such advice. Touche Ross would be pleased to advise on any problems that arise.

While all reasonable care has been taken in the preparation of this book, no responsibility is accepted by the author, or by Touche Ross, for any errors it may contain, whether caused by negligence or otherwise, or for any loss, howsoever caused, occasioned to any person by reliance on it.

Touche Ross & Co. in Great Britain and Touche Ross & Co. in the Channel Islands are each authorised to carry on Investment Business by the Institute of Chartered Accountants in England & Wales, and Touche Ross & Co. in Northern Ireland is authorised to carry on Investment Business by the Institute of Chartered Accountants in Ireland.

February 1989

THE AUTHOR –
DEREK A. ROSS

BSc, LLB, FCA, FTII, ACMA, FCT

On graduation in 1971, Derek Ross trained with Touche Ross and, after some years managing audits of international companies, he transferred to the firm's management consultancy, where he specialised in corporate rescue and banking.

In 1977, he moved to Black and Decker in Belgium where he started his career as a treasurer, becoming European Treasurer and Tax Manager.

In 1983, he returned to the UK to set up the treasury consulting operation for Touche Ross. He manages a team of thirteen corporate treasurers and has undertaken a wide range of projects in industry and the public sector.

Derek Ross is the author of the textbook *International Treasury Management*. He is an active member of the Association of Corporate Treasurers and serves as Chairman of the Technical Committee and as a member of the Council.

[1]

INTRODUCTION

This book explains the UK taxation law and practice of contemporary financial transactions and instruments. It deals only with their treatment for corporation tax purposes, since individuals or unincorporated traders are unlikely to enter into such transactions in anything like the volume companies do. Although addressing primarily the UK tax issues, international comments are made where these are relevant to the application of UK revenue law, for example in relation to double tax relief or the provisions of certain of the UK's Double Tax Treaties.

The text is believed to reflect the law and practice of UK taxation as it applied on 31 December 1988.

[2]
GENERAL FEATURES OF THE UK TAX SYSTEM

2.1 Background

Financial trading in new instruments such as futures, options, interest rate agreements of various types, and in some not so new transactions, such as foreign exchange, has grown to massive proportions. Notwithstanding the amount of money involved and the huge profits and losses being made, the amount of UK tax law on the subject remains tiny, much being left to Revenue practice. This state of affairs results in uncertainty.

The essence of a good tax system is certainty. A taxpayer should be able to know in advance with reasonable certainty what the outcome of his transactions will be.

Some of the general features of the UK tax system that do not sit comfortably with modern business practice are set out below. The impact of specific features of particular transactions are dealt with, as appropriate, in subsequent chapters.

2.2 Groups

Most major businesses are groups of companies. A group is usually managed as one economic entity. The separate legal personalities of individual companies often only exist for technical or practical reasons. UK Revenue law is based on separate companies with an overlay of provisions, reliefs, elections and anti-avoidance law applied to accommodate groups. In other words, tax is not applied and computed on a total UK group basis. Consequentially, certain anomalies exist. For example, although subsidiaries' contemporaneous trading losses can be transferred to other group companies, capital losses cannot. Another example is that the new statement of practice on foreign exchange gains or losses (*see* section 3.5) is applicable company by company only. Although the Revenue appreciates that groups manage foreign exchange on a consolidated basis, it was impossible to produce a workable solution on this principle within the current structure of UK Revenue law.

As a result, the overall tax effect will depend on how a group's foreign exchange transactions are spread around the UK group, even though this is irrelevant to the consolidated pre-tax profits.

2.3   Capital and Revenue

UK law distinguishes items of a capital and revenue nature. This can produce some bizarre results. For example, if a business raises money, it is reasonable to expect that the total cost of servicing the debt should be deductible.

Under general tax law, if a company borrows in foreign currency and the loan is long term, gains and losses on repayment may not be taxable or relievable. This is because the loan is likely to be regarded as a capital item and the gain or loss is therefore not of a revenue nature. As far as the corporation tax charge on capital gains is concerned, this tax applies to the disposal of a chargeable asset, not to the satisfaction of a liability. Thus, the item falls out of the tax net altogether, even though economically the foreign exchange gain or loss is part of the cost of the finance, since the exchange risk is reflected in the interest rate. Strong currencies have low rates but a greater chance of exchange loss if they are borrowed. Weak currency borrowings are likely to produce exchange gains on repayment but have higher interest rates.

2.4   Tax Status of Companies

UK revenue law treats the same transaction differently depending on its tax status within the company. Financial transactions will almost certainly be included in the Schedule

D Case I computation of companies, mostly banks, engaged in financial trade.

The same transaction may be treated differently by a general trading company and differently again by an investment company. This whole problem, when related to the one of groups, can have potentially disastrous consequences.

For example, many PLCs are investment companies. They are the holding company for a group of trading companies, although not themselves trading companies. Unlike trading companies, which can deduct any expenses incurred wholly and exclusively for the purposes of their trade, investment companies can only obtain a tax deduction for certain specified expenses. If, therefore, an investment company borrows money to finance group operations and then makes a payment to provide interest rate protection (known as an interest rate guarantee, *see* chapter 13), the cost of this protection cannot be tax deducted under any provision of current tax law.

2.5   Interest

UK law on interest is complex. It is different depending on the length of the debt, the type of borrower and the type of lender. The general provisions relating to interest are set out more fully in chapter 6. These provisions are not well suited to modern transactions.

For example, many interest rate management techniques such as swaps (chapter 11), forward rate agreements (chapter 12) and interest rate guarantees (chapter 13), involve payments that are economically equivalent to interest. They are computed by reference to interest rates. However, because an underlying debtor/creditor relationship does not exist, UK law cannot treat them as interest. This produces anomalous results.

[3]

FOREIGN EXCHANGE GAINS AND LOSSES

3.1   Introduction

In the UK, as in many other jurisdictions, there is little legislation dealing with the taxation of foreign exchange gains and losses. For example, as regards the computation of Schedule D Case I profits, the only statutory provision is that 'sums paid in consequence of, or for obtaining protection against, losses resulting from changes in the rate of exchange between different currencies' shall not be deductible as an incidental cost of obtaining loan finance (TA 1988 s.77(7)). By implication, such sums are not deductible for any other purpose by a company, unless the company is trading in the relevant instruments.

It has therefore fallen to the Courts to derive a system for taxing currency fluctuations from the basic principles of UK taxation. This they have done. Accordingly, exchange gains and losses may be brought into the Case I computation only if they arise in the course of trading operations. So, for example, foreign currency trade account receivables will give rise to revenue gains or losses which must be brought into the Case I computation. On the other hand, a currency transaction connected with, say, the sale of foreign land will give rise to gains or losses on capital account. These must be excluded from the Case I computation, but they may be taxed or relieved under the capital gains tax legislation. Gains or losses on a currency hedge will normally be taxed or relieved according to the nature of the underlying transaction.

It has also been established that neither gains nor losses may be anticipated for tax purposes. Therefore, only realised gains or losses should be brought into the Case I computation. Clearly, gains or losses arising on currency conversion transactions will always be realised and must be taxed or relieved accordingly.

Gains or losses arising on translation would not normally be regarded as realised. Nevertheless, where accounts are kept in foreign currency and translated into sterling using the 'balance sheet', or 'temporal', method (where *current* assets and liabilities are valued at the opening and closing balance sheet dates at the exchange rates then prevailing), any gains or losses arising from that translation will be brought into the Case I computation. In practice, the Inland Revenue has long accepted computations including unrealised gains and losses on trading items, provided both gains and losses are recognised, and provided also that computations are prepared on a consistent basis from year to year.

3.2   Pattison v. Marine Midland Ltd

The anomalies produced by the application of these principles were highlighted in *Pattison* v. *Marine Midland Ltd* [1984] STC 10. The taxpayer company raised US$15 m (then equivalent to £6 m) by the issue of dollar subordinated loan stock. The funds so raised were kept in dollars. They were used in the ordinary course of the company's banking business to make advances in dollars. The taxpayer's intention was to maintain, so far as possible, a matched currency position. When the loan stock was repaid, payment was made out of the company's dollar funds. On repayment the US$15 m was then the equivalent of £8.6 m.

The Inland Revenue contended that there had been an exchange loss of £2.6 m on the loan stock and a corresponding exchange gain on the dollar banking assets which the loan stock had financed. The Revenue argued that the loan stock formed part of the company's capital structure. It did not therefore give rise to a revenue deduction. The exchange gain, on the other hand, arose on the company's banking assets and so fell to be taxed as income. The taxpayer, of course, argued that since the assets and liabilities had been maintained in dollars, no exchange gains and losses had arisen.

The House of Lords found for Marine Midland. It held that neither gain nor loss had arisen for tax purposes on the lending or borrowing. A gain or loss might have arisen on the conversion of dollars into some other currency, but there was no such gain or loss because the company did not make any relevant currency conversions.

> Lord Templeman: 'The Crown's argument that the company made a capital loss on its unsecured loan stock and an income profit on its customers' borrowing is misconceived. There never was any loss or profit from the lending and borrowing and there never was any exchange profit because the company did not make any relevant currency conversions'.

Their Lordships did not comment on whether the loan stock should properly be categorised as capital when the funds raised were put to a revenue purpose. However, in *Beauchamp* v. *F. W. Woolworth plc* [1988] STI 622, the Court of Appeal held that the basic principle in regard to loans is that they are revenue in nature only if they are a means of fluctuating and temporary accommodation. In determining the nature of the accommodation, regard may be had not only to the terms of the loan but also to the taxpayer's purpose in raising it. Only in doubtful cases, however, will the use which is actually made of borrowed money throw any light on the nature of the borrowing.

3.3   The Revenue's Reaction

Following the House of Lord's decision in Marine Midland, the Inland Revenue issued a Provisional Statement of Practice, SP3/85. This was followed by a definitive Statement of Practice, SP1/87, intended 'as a general guide to facilitate the preparation and agreement of tax computations of *trading taxpayers*'.

The Inland Revenue expects taxpayers to comply with the Statement of Practice. In an exceptional case, where some other basis of computation is used, the taxpayer will have to justify the case for special treatment to his inspector. For this reason, the remainder of this section will concentrate, so far as is relevant, on the terms of SP1/87.

There is a considerable body of opinion (to which the author subscribes) that SP1/87 is based on a fundamental misunderstanding of the Marine Midland decision. SP1/87 is based on the assumption that the case turned on there being no exchange gain on the assets because they were matched with liabilities. The better view, it is contended, is that the case turned on there having been no relevant currency conversions. The fact that the assets and liabilities were matched was merely a consequence of this.

3.4   Accountancy Practice

Perhaps the keystone of the Inland Revenue's approach following Marine Midland is the view expressed in paragraphs 8 and 9 of SP1/87. This states that where accounts are compiled in accordance with the Companies Acts and generally accepted accountancy principles, then those accounts should incorporate translation profits and losses. Such profits and losses should also be taken into account for tax purposes, unless they are in respect of capital items or there are other particular reasons for excluding them. In deciding what is generally accepted accountancy practice for this purpose, the Revenue will pay particular regard to Statement of Standard Accounting Practice 20: *Foreign Currency Translation* (SSAP 20) and to published accounting practices of particular industries.

SSAP 20 requires, in general, that each asset, liability, revenue or cost arising from a transaction denominated in a foreign currency should be translated into the company's local currency at the exchange rate prevailing at the date of the transaction. Local currency is defined as 'the currency of the primary economic environment in which the business operates and generates net cash flows'. Where the transaction is to be settled at a contracted rate, that contracted rate should be used, and where a trading transaction is hedged by a forward contract, the forward contract rate may be used.

Once non-monetary assets, for example, plant, machinery and equity investments, have been translated and recorded, they should be carried in the company's local currency so that unrealised gains and losses on such assets will not normally be recognised. Monetary assets and liabilities, for example, cash and bank balances, loans and amounts receivable and payable, which are denominated in foreign currency, should be translated at the balance sheet date, generally using the rate prevailing on that date. However, where there are related or matching forward contracts in respect of trading transactions, the rates of exchange specified in those contracts may be used.

As a rule, both realised and unrealised exchange gains and losses should be recognised in the profit and loss account, rather than taken directly through reserves. Exceptionally, however, where foreign currency borrowings have been used to finance foreign currency equity investment, both borrowings and investment may be translated as at the balance sheet date and any exchange differences taken direct to reserves, without passing through the profit and loss account.

Further detailed rules apply when preparing consolidated accounts for a company and its foreign branches or subsidiaries. Broadly, unless the foreign enterprise is merely an extension of its head office, translational differences will be recorded only as movements on reserves.

3.5   Statement of Practice SP1/87

In outlining its post-Marine Midland approach to exchange gains and losses, the Inland Revenue maintains the continued importance of the distinction between capital and revenue, particularly in determining the chargeability and deductibility of exchange gains and losses on foreign currency loans.

That distinction, it is said, 'is essentially between loans providing temporary financial accommodation and loans which can be said to add to the capital of the business'.

Nevertheless, the Revenue finds authority in Marine Midland for the view that the capital or revenue nature of borrowings ceases to be relevant where those borrowings are matched by assets in the same currency. Accordingly, to the extent that foreign currency denominated monetary assets are equalled by liabilities in the same currency, so that a translation adjustment on one would be cancelled out by a translation adjustment on the other, no adjustments should be made in computing trading profits or losses for tax purposes.

Since UK corporation tax recognises groups of companies only for the purposes of certain specified reliefs, the matching principle must be applied on a company-by-company basis. This can produce major problems for groups of companies that are economically managed as one entity. Here, a central treasury function may match the group's foreign exchange position, even though individual companies may remain exposed with unmatched positions. This modern management style cannot be accommodated by either existing law or SP1/87.

3.6   Unmatched Positions

Where a company's foreign currency monetary assets and liabilities are not matched throughout an accounting period, some adjustment will be required in computing its Case I profits. This will be in respect of exchange gains and losses credited or debited to profit and loss account in respect of capital items. Clearly, it will normally be impracticable to seek to apply the matching concept on a day-to-day basis. The Revenue, therefore, offers an alternative practice which may be adopted, provided it is applied consistently from year to year. Where it is not consistently applied, capital assets and liabilities will be regarded as matched only to the extent that matching can be demonstrated by reference to the trader's currency assets and liabilities during the period.

The Revenue's preferred practice assumes that:

- the extent to which foreign currency monetary assets and liabilities are matched during an accounting period is reflected in the net exchange difference taken to profit and loss account or, in some circumstances, to reserves; and

- capital liabilities are matched primarily with capital assets in the same currency, and then with current assets in that currency, but only to the extent that those current assets exceed current liabilities in the relevant currency.

Accordingly, where there is neither a net exchange gain nor a net exchange loss on capital items, no adjustment will be required in computing the Case I profit. Similarly, no adjustment is needed if either:

- there is a net exchange gain on capital items and an overall net exchange loss charged to profit and loss account; or

- there is a net exchange loss on capital items and an overall net exchange gain credited to profit and loss account.

Where, however, there is a net exchange gain on capital items and an overall net exchange gain credited to profit and loss account, the smaller of those net gains shall be treated as not taxable and the appropriate adjustment made in the Case I computation.

Likewise, where there is a net exchange loss on capital items and an overall net exchange loss charged to profit and loss account, the smaller of those two losses must be added back in the Case I computation. It follows that the adjustment required in respect of capital items will not exceed the overall net exchange difference taken to profit and loss account.

3.7   Currency Swaps

In general, where there are transactions in more than one currency, the practice described above must be applied to each currency separately. Where a trader enters into a currency swap, exchanging borrowed currency for an equivalent amount of another currency (including sterling) for a fixed period, the two transactions in the original currency must be matched, effectively converting the original liability to a liability in the second currency for the duration of the swap.

If, when the swap is terminated, the currencies are swapped back at the exchange rate prevailing at the commencement of the swap, there will be neither profit nor loss for Case I purposes in terms of the original currency, although the capital gains consequences of that transaction will need to be considered. (*See* section 5.2 for further details on this point.)

3.8 Hedging Transactions

A hedging transaction is one entered into to protect the value of another transaction from the effect of a movement in financial variables such as interest or exchange rates. For example, if goods are sold in dollars to a US customer for $100m when the rate is £1 = $1.80, the company is exposed to loss if the dollar falls to, say £1 = $1.90. A hedging transaction might be a forward sale of dollars to protect the value in sterling of the dollar receivable.

Where an otherwise unmatched position in a particular currency is hedged using forward exchange contracts, or currency futures, the Revenue will accept that the position is matched for tax purposes, provided the hedge is reflected in the accounts on a consistent basis from year to year and in accordance with accepted accountancy practice. For example, a trading transaction hedged by a forward currency contract may be translated under SSAP 20 at the rate specified in the forward contract.

On the other hand, the Revenue does not accept that a currency position can be matched for tax purposes by a currency option based hedge (*see* chapter 4).

3.9 Overseas Branches and Trades

Where a trade carried on wholly abroad, or an overseas branch, has a local currency other than sterling, accounts will normally be prepared in that currency. These must be translated to produce a taxable (Case I) profit expressed in sterling. In these circumstances, the Revenue will accept computations based on:

- accounts prepared in the local currency, with the adjusted profit before capital allowances and other statutory reliefs and charges, translated into sterling either at the average rate for the accounting period or at the closing rate for that period; or

- the sterling equivalent of accounts prepared in local currency, translated into sterling using the 'net invest-ment/closing rate' method. This means, broadly, that balance sheet items are translated at the rate ruling at the balance sheet date and profit and loss account items either at the closing rate or at an average rate for the accounting period; or

- sterling accounts produced by the 'temporal' method, where each transaction is recorded in sterling equivalent at the date it occurs.

Whichever method is chosen, it must be applied consistently. It will affect only the Case I profit before capital allowances and any other statutory reliefs and charges. These must be computed in sterling, converting from the local currency at the exchange rate in force when the relevant expenditure was incurred (*see also* section 3.13 below). The tax treatment of any exchange gains and losses reflected in the local foreign currency accounts must, of course, be determined according to the principles set out in SP1/87.

3.10 Realisation Basis

Some financial concerns hold assets, other than stock, which when disposed of may give rise to profits. Such profits will be taxed as trading profits. Although the assets, while held, cannot be revalued at the lower of cost or net realisable value, it is normal accounting practice to revalue them to reflect currency fluctuations. Where the resulting exchange gains or losses are taken to profit and loss account, or are set off against exchange gains or losses on liabilities as part of the matching process, the Revenue will normally follow the accounts treatment for tax purposes, provided it is applied consistently. The treatment, though, of any given case will be for agreement with the Inspector.

3.11 Roundabouts

As noted above, exchange gains and losses on borrowings can only be brought into a borrower's Case I computations where the liability is short term and on revenue account. In the past, however, a number of companies sought to secure Case I treatment for currency fluctuations on long-term borrowings, by having an offshore associated company incur the long-term liability and then on lend to the UK, short term.

SP1/87 notes that where the UK company has a matched currency position, no Case I adjustment will now be required whether its borrowing is long or short term. To that extent, the Revenue expects such 'roundabout' arrangements to fall into disuse. Where they are still used in an unmatched, or partly matched situation, the Revenue may invoke the 'Ramsay doctrine' (*see W. T. Ramsay Ltd* v. *IRC* [1982] STC 30; *Furniss* v. *Dawson* [1984] STC 153; and *Craven* v. *White* [1988] STC 476). They will treat the finance raised by the UK trader as raised on the terms applicable to its associate's long-term borrowing. The Revenue has stated, however, that it will not interfere with arrangements already in place on 17 February 1987, unless they are renegotiated after that date (SP1/87 para. 30).

3.12   Non-trading Companies

The Inland Revenue does not regard the Marine Midland decision as having any relevance outside the trading context. Accordingly, where a non-trading company engages in foreign currency transactions, its gains and losses will be taxed or allowed (if at all) under the capital gains regime (*see* section 3.14) unless, exceptionally, they fall within Schedule D Case VI.

Tax under Case VI is charged in respect of any annual profits or gains not falling under any other Case of Schedule D and not charged by virtue of Schedule A, B, C or E, and on any other income specifically directed by statute to be charged under Case VI (TA 1988 s.18).

None of the many items specifically charged under Case VI relate directly to currency fluctuations. Should an exchange gain or loss arise as part of an item so charged (for example, income from UK furnished lettings where the rents are received in dollars), then an element of currency fluctuations will be reflected in the taxable income.

As regards the general mopping up nature of Case VI, it should be noted that a profit derived from an isolated transaction of purchase and resale is not within the Case (*Leeming* v. *Jones* [1930] 15 TC 333). It follows that the only currency transactions exposed to Case VI are speculations in the futures market, although even these are now often taxed as capital transactions (*see* chapters 10 and 4 on futures and traded options).

3.13   Capital Allowances

Capital allowances are given in respect of capital expenditure incurred by a trading taxpayer on the provision of certain 'qualifying assets' (notably plant and machinery, factories and other industrial buildings) for the purposes of his trade. Entitlement to capital allowances generally arises on the date on which the relevant expenditure is incurred. That is taken to be the date on which the obligation to pay becomes unconditional, whether or not there is a later date on which the whole or part of the sum due must be paid. The expenditure will normally be incurred on the date on which title to the asset in question passes to the purchaser (FA 1985 s.56).

As a general rule, if the price of the qualifying asset is denominated in foreign currency, the sterling cost upon which allowances will be based must be computed at the exchange rate ruling when the expenditure is incurred (Inland Revenue Press Release of 6 October 1976). Where, however, the purchase contract provides for deferred payment, any exchange gain or loss arising throughout the credit period will be relevant in calculating the amount eligible for allowances (*Van Arkadie* v. *Sterling Coated Materials Ltd* [1983] STC 95).

On the other hand, if the purchase is funded out of borrowings, any additional sterling cost incurred in repaying those borrowings will not attract allowances. This is because it is not expenditure on the provision of the relevant asset (*Ben-Odeco* v. *Powlson* [1978] STC 460). Neither will such additional cost qualify for any other relief or deduction.

Once the sterling cost of an asset is determined, this fixes the basis of computation of all future capital allowances.

Subsequent movements in the sterling value of the asset are therefore irrelevant for tax purposes.

3.14 Capital Gains

Foreign currency is a chargeable asset for the purpose of capital gains tax (CGTA 1979 s.19(1)(b); TA 1988 s.345(2)). Accordingly, gains and losses arising on a disposal of foreign currency are chargeable gains or allowable losses. There is one exception – if the currency was acquired by an individual for his personal expenditure (or that of his family or dependants) outside the UK (CGTA 1979 s.133).

Furthermore, foreign currency bank accounts are distinguished from ordinary debts. Whereas a debt is not normally a chargeable asset in the hands of the original creditor, unless it is a 'debt on a security' as defined, a chargeable gain or allowable loss may arise on the disposal of currency out of a foreign currency bank account. Here again there is the exception for personal expenditure (CGTA 1979 s.135).

For these purposes, currency is disposed of either by its conversion or by its expenditure, for example on the purchase of some other asset. Strictly, direct transfers from one foreign currency bank account to another involve both the disposal and acquisition of assets.

By concession, a taxpayer may treat all bank accounts in his name containing the same currency as one account. He may, therefore, ignore transfers between them. Once adopted, this practice must be applied to all future transfers between the taxpayer's accounts containing the relevant currency, until the whole of the debt represented in the bank accounts has been repaid (Inland Revenue Statement of Practice SP10/84).

Like shares and securities, foreign currency is a fungible asset. This means that it is not possible to distinguish between, say, one US dollar and another, so that the one may be freely substituted for the other without legal or commercial effect. Consequently, special rules are needed to determine which of a person's dollars (for example) have been disposed of, their acquisition cost and the date from which the capital gains indexation allowance will run. The rules applied are the same as those that apply to shares and securities (FA 1985 s.68(9)(b)).

Any detailed consideration of these complex rules is beyond the scope of this book. Broadly, however, a person's holdings of any given currency are treated as forming a single asset which grows or diminishes as acquisitions or disposals of that currency are made. A disposal of currency must first be identified with any acquisition of the same currency on the same day, then with acquisitions of that currency in the previous ten days, and only then with the relevant currency 'pool'.

For capital gains purposes, an asset acquired or disposed of under a contract is treated as acquired or disposed of on the date of that contract (or, if conditional, on the date on which it becomes unconditional) and *not* on the date of its completion (CGTA 1979 s.27). So, for example, currency bought forward will be treated as acquired on the date the forward contract is entered into and not when the currency is delivered under the contract.

It follows from the above that where foreign currency is used to purchase a foreign currency asset, there is both a disposal of the currency (which may give rise to a chargeable gain or allowable loss) and an acquisition of the asset purchased, at the same value. When the asset is later sold for foreign currency, there is a disposal of the asset and an acquisition of currency, again at the same value. A third disposal will occur when the sale proceeds of the asset are, say, converted into sterling.

When computing the gain or loss arising on the disposal of an asset denominated in foreign currency, its acquisition cost and disposal proceeds must be translated into sterling at the date of acquisition or disposal as the case may be (applying the contract date where relevant). It is not permissible to compute the gain or loss in foreign currency and then to translate the net figure into sterling (*Bentley* v. *Pike* [1981] STC 360).

Even where foreign currency is borrowed to acquire an asset, the expenditure of the borrowed funds on the asset will constitute the disposal of currency for capital gains purposes and the position will be broadly as described above. Any gain

17

or loss in sterling terms on the repayment of a long-term capital loan cannot be brought into account for capital gains purposes. This is because the satisfaction of a liability is not the disposal of an asset.

[4]
CURRENCY AND OTHER OPTIONS

4.1 Background

Financial options are contracts that give the right, but not the obligation, to purchase (call) or sell (put) an agreed amount of a financial instrument at a particular price (known as the strike price) for a particular length of time.

Options may be on currencies, financial futures, commodities, or any other financial instrument or security. Options are of two types:

- they may be exchange traded, for example, on the London and Philadelphia Stock Exchanges, London International Financial Futures Exchange (LIFFE), the Chicago Futures Exchange; or

- they may be written specifically, normally by a bank. These are called over-the-counter options.

Taking the case of foreign currency options, the advantage of using this hedging technique is that, unlike transactions such as forward contracts, they do not fix a particular exchange rate. Instead they set a limit to the rate. Thus, rather than sell a dollar receivable at a forward rate of £1 = $1.80, which would be disadvantageous if sterling fell to £1 = $1.70, an option to sell dollars at £1 = $1.80 could be purchased. The option would not be exercised if sterling fell. In this circumstance the option would be abandoned, but a gain would arise on the receivable.

The option would protect the sterling amount of the dollar receivable if sterling rose to, say £1 = $1.90. The loss on the conversion of the dollar receivable at £1 = $1.90 would be offset by the 10-cent profit on the exercise of the option. The premium paid for the option would represent the cost of the hedge.

The major volume of options business is exchange traded. Sections 4.2 and 4.3 deal in detail with the taxation of traded options. The treatment of certain over-the-counter options has now been brought into line with traded options and this is dealt with in section 4.4.

4.2 Basis of Taxation – Trading Transactions

Where a bank or other financial trader deals in traded options, the profits or losses arising will form part of the Schedule D Case I results of its financial trade unless, exceptionally, they arise on dealings in options intended to hedge transactions on capital account. In this case they will be taxed as capital profits or losses.

A company which deals in options for profit may also be taxed on its dealing profits and losses under Schedule D Case I, if those dealings amount to the carrying on of a trade or to an adventure in the nature of the trade. This is a question of fact dependent on all the traditional 'badges of trade' – largely on the number of transactions carried out; the expertise of the 'trader', whether staff are employed, whether dealing decisions are made by the 'trader' or left to a broker, and whether the deals are financed by way of loan. The Inland Revenue has stated that a company will not be regarded as trading for these purposes if the transactions are relatively infrequent or where, for example, the intention is to hedge specific investments (*see* SP4/88, (1988) ST1 590).

Finally, a company other than a financial trader which deals in options wholly to hedge transactions on revenue account, such as the example above, to protect a trading receivable, may also bring its profits or losses on the hedge into the computation of taxable profits of the underlying trade (*see* SP4/88 para. 11).

Where dealings in options do fall to be taxed under Schedule D Case I, the profit or loss should, as a general rule, be computed on a realisations basis. This is because neither profit nor loss should be anticipated for tax purposes. Where contracts which are open at the end of the accounting period are brought into account at their market value, the Revenue will, in practice, accept the same approach for tax purposes, provided both profit- and loss-making contracts are marked to market and provided also that the same treatment is applied consistently from year to year.

Should a company wish to be taxed on a realisations basis, profits and losses realised at the year end (but deferred in the accounts until the profit and loss on the hedged transaction is recognised) must be brought into account for tax purposes in the period of realisation.

4.3   Basis of Taxation – Non-trading Transactions

Prior to 6 April 1985, profits and losses arising from transactions in traded options not forming part of a trade were normally taxed as income profits and losses under Schedule D Case VI. This meant that losses were relievable only against Case VI profits of the same or later years in the same company. This applied even when options were used to hedge capital transactions. Since that date, however, such profits and losses have been taxed as capital gains and losses, provided they have arisen from transactions on LIFFE or on any other options exchange in the UK, or elsewhere, which is recognised by the Inland Revenue or on a recognised stock exchange (FA 1985 s.72 and TA 1988 ss.128 and 399(1), (5)). Indeed, since 2 July 1986 options on gilts and qualifying corporate bonds have been exempt even that charge (FA 1986 s.59).

The capital gains treatment of traded options is as follows:

- If the option moves out of the money, it will not be exercised and its holder will be treated as abandoning it on the last possible exercise date. This gives rise to an allowable loss equal to the premium paid for the option together with any incidental costs and indexation allowance (CGTA 1979 ss.137(4), 138). Unlike other options, traded options are not wasting assets and the whole of their cost may be deducted in computing the gain or loss on their disposal.

21

- If, on the other hand, the option is exercised, the acquisition of the option and the transaction entered into on its exercise are treated as a single transaction. Accordingly, relief for the premium paid for the option will be given only when the underlying transaction is closed out (CGTA 1979 s.137(3)). Thus the cost of a call option, say on an equity, will be added to the cost of the shares and allowed when the shares are disposed of. Similarly, the cost of a put option will be regarded as an addition to the allowable expenditure on the shares sold under the put option at the option's strike price. The strike price also represents the consideration on disposal. In each case, the capital gains indexation allowance will run on the option premium from the date of acquisition of the option and on its exercise price from the date of exercise.

Where, exceptionally, a traded option is written otherwise than as part of the grantor's trade, similar treatment will apply to the grantor. The grant of the option will rank as a disposal giving rise to a gain equal to the premium received, less incidental costs (CGTA 1979 s.137(1)). If the option is *not* exercised, no further gain or loss will arise. If the option *is* exercised, its grant and its exercise must be treated as a single transaction and the premium received on the grant brought into the computation of the gain or loss arising when the underlying contract is completed. Any tax previously paid in respect of the grant of the option will be repayable (CGTA 1979 s.137(2)).

There are no statutory provisions, similar to those in FA 1985 s.72(3) which apply to futures, that could treat the writer of an option as disposing of it when he or she closes out his or her position by the purchase of an identical option. Nevertheless, such an approach might be acceptable in practice, particularly where the clearing house regards the taxpayer as having no open position.

4.4 Recent Developments in Over-the-counter Options

With effect from 29 April 1988, the tax treatment of over-the-counter dealings in *financial options* has been brought into line with that of traded options described above (F[No.2]A 1987 s.81 as brought into force by SI No. 74 of 1988).

Thus, provided they do not take place in the course of a trade, over-the-counter transactions in financial futures will be taxed as capital rather than income transactions. Broadly:

- gains from such transactions will be taxed as capital provided they do not form part of a trade (F[No.2]A 1987 s.81(1), (2));

- the abandonment of any such options will constitute a disposal of them, giving rise to chargeable gains or allowable losses (F[No.2]A 1987 s.81(4));

- such options will *not* be treated as wasting assets and the whole of their cost will be deductible in computing the gains or losses arising on disposal (F[No.2]A 1987 s.81(6), (7)).

For these purposes, 'financial options' include over-the-counter options:

- in currency, shares, securities or interest rates instruments granted by a member of a recognised stock exchange;

- in shares or securities traded on a recognised stock exchange, granted to or by a member of such an exchange, either as principal or agent (F[No.2]A 1987 s.81(5)).

Further, in its Statement of Practice SP4/88, published on 25 July 1988, the Inland Revenue confirmed that where a transaction in financial futures or options is clearly related to an underlying transaction, asset or portfolio, the tax treatment of the futures or option contract will follow that of the underlying transaction, asset or portfolio. Such a relationship is regarded as existing where the futures or options are used as a hedge to reduce the risk attaching to the underlying transaction, asset or portfolio.

A transaction will be treated as a hedge for these purposes if:

(a) it is economically appropriate to the reduction in risk of the underlying transaction, asset or portfolio; and

(b) the price fluctuations of the options or futures are directly and demonstrably related to the fluctuations in value or composition of the underlying transaction, asset or portfolio, at the time the hedge is initiated.

This treatment applies to all futures and options, whether traded on an exchange or otherwise.

[5]

CURRENCY SWAPS

5.1   Explanation of Transaction

Accessibility in the market to the cheapest source of funds is the commercial rationale for the currency swap transaction.

Example A

Suppose that a US company, X, wishes to borrow sterling to hedge the exposure on translating the sterling accounts of its UK subsidiary into dollars. Assume also that a UK company, Y, may wish to borrow dollars to hedge the exposure of its US subsidiary. It may be cheaper for X to borrow dollars than Y. Similarly, it may be cheaper for Y to borrow sterling. These borrowings will be undertaken and then X and Y will swap their debt obligations. The swap will be reversed in, say, four years. During the life of the swap a payment will be made from X to Y if sterling interest rates remain higher than dollar ones. This represents the interest differential.

This swap is similar to a long-term foreign exchange contract. The UK company has swapped its sterling liability for a dollar liability, but in four years' time it must repay the dollars it owes to the US company. It will then receive sterling in return.

Suppose the exchange rate is £1 = $2 at the inception of the swap and £1 = $1 on reversal in four years.

Now:

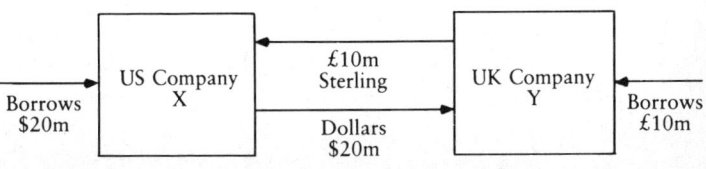

At end of swap:

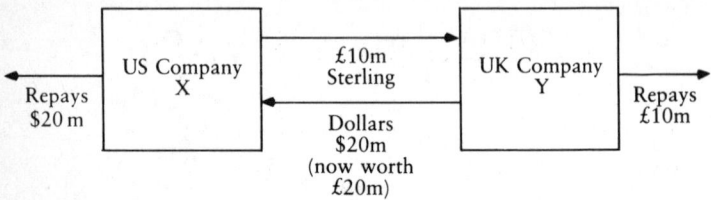

In commercial terms Y has lost £10m on the swap, because it receives £10m from X but must pay $20m (now worth £20m) to X. The overall commercial effect depends on what a UK company did with the dollars when it first received them. For example, if it acquired a dollar asset, or even if it just left the dollars in a bank account, then the dollar asset or the dollars would have increased in sterling value to £20m and the profit on the asset (only a gain if realised by disposing of the asset) or the dollars would be equal to the loss on the swap.

Example B

Suppose that a UK company, Y, actually wishes to raise sterling. Because of a temporary arbitrage opportunity, it is possible to borrow dollars and swap them into sterling at a saving in interest. A bank organises the transaction with counterparty X, a company wishing to raise dollar debt. X could be resident anywhere.

Now:

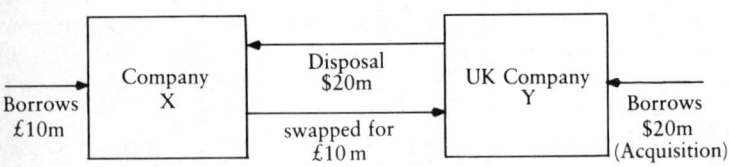

At end of swap:

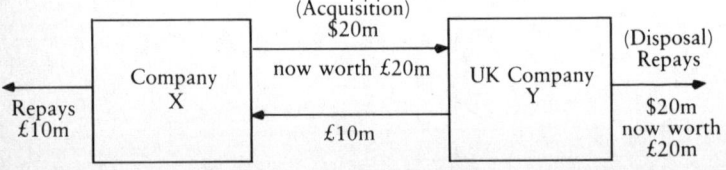

At the outset, $20m (worth £10m) has been acquired from the loan.

Also at the outset, there has been a disposal to X of $20m (worth £10m) together with a contract to acquire $20m in, say, five years for consideration of £10m.

On reversal of the swap, although the acquisition cost of the $20m is £10m under the contract, these dollars are disposed of to repay the loan, the disposal proceeds being £20m. For tax purposes there is a 'gain' on the swap of £10m and a loss on the borrowing of £10m. In commercial terms the transactions are matched.

If sterling interest rates are higher than dollar rates, then during the swap, compensatory payments will be made by Y to X.

5.2   Tax Implications

In order to determine the tax implications of the currency swap, it is necessary to look at each part of the transaction.

As far as recent cases on anti-avoidance are concerned (notably *Ramsay* v. *IRC* [1982] STC 30; *Furniss* v. *Dawson* [1984] STC 153; and *Craven* v. *White* [1988] STC 476), the Revenue may now look at a transaction in its entirety. This new principle, however, cannot be extended to all tax issues.

5.2.1   *Interest Differential Payments*

Interest differential payments between parties are computed by reference to the difference in interest rates. They are not, therefore, regarded as payments of interest for taxation purposes. Since currency swaps are usually long-term transactions, they are normally regarded as annual payments and this gives rise to a different tax treatment from interest. The treatment is discussed in detail in section 12.2, which deals with compensatory payments under interest rate swap agreements. The tax law is the same for both transactions and so is not repeated here.

5.2.2   *Set-up Costs*

Set-up costs will normally be paid, probably to a bank. As the law presently stands, these are not regarded as incidental costs of obtaining loan finance. This means that non-banking companies may not obtain a tax deduction for these costs. (*See* section 11.3 for further details).

5.2.3 *Currency Gains and Losses*

There is no currency effect at the outset of a currency swap. This is because the counterparties have just swapped their debt obligations. It is on the reversal of the swap that a foreign currency gain or loss is most likely be realised.

For trading taxpayers, the Schedule D Case I consequences of the transaction are now dealt with by Statement of Practice SP1/87 (*see* section 3.7). We must, therefore, look at what the Statement of Practice has to say about swaps.

Paragraph 23 begins with the words:

> Where a trader enters into a currency swap agreement to exchange borrowed currency for an equivalent amount of another currency for a fixed period, the two transactions in the original currency should be treated as matched, so that the underlying liability in the first currency is effectively converted into a liability in the second currency for the duration of the swap.

If this applied to Example B, the intention seems to permit matching a dollar borrowing with the dollar leg of the swap, although the wording is unclear.

In tax terms, on maturity Company Y has received a gain of £10m on the unwinding of the swap and an equal loss in sterling on repaying the dollar borrowing. Assume that both transactions are on capital account. Prima facie, the gain on the swap would be subject to corporation tax as a capital gain, while the loss on the repayment of the borrowing would not be deductible.

Paragraph 23, in the provisional version of the Statement of Practice, concluded:

> If when the swap is terminated the currencies are swapped back at the spot rate of exchange prevailing at the commencement of the swap there will be no exchange loss or profit *for Case I* purposes.

There is, of course, no exchange loss or profit for Case I or any other purpose on the unwinding of the swap. However, there is still a gain or loss on the disposal of the dollars. The issue is whether the currency is used to repay the borrowing or whether the transactions are treated as matched.

Paragraph 23 only mentions Case I and does not cover the capital gains consequences. Thus, there may be a charge to corporation tax on the swap (asset) leg of the transaction without a deduction for the loss on the borrowing (liability) leg. The final version of the Statement of Practice implicity acknowledges this problem by adding the words:

> (but the capital gains consequences of unwinding the swap will need to be taken into account).

The result of this inequity is not always to the taxpayer's disadvantage. It appears in Example B above, that there is a chargeable gain on the swap because of the disposal of the dollars to repay the loan, but there is no allowable deduction on the loan itself. If the dollar had in fact fallen to £1 = $4, then on reversal of the swap, $20m would have been acquired for £10m and immediately disposed of to repay the loan for £5m, realising an allowable capital loss of £5m. On the other hand, the $20m loan originally worth £10m would have been repaid for £5m, but this gain, being on a capital liability, would *not* be subject to tax.

[6]

LOAN FINANCE – MAIN TAX ISSUES

6.1 Interest Deductibility

6.1.1 *Relief for Interest Paid*

Short interest can be defined, broadly, as interest on a temporary facility not intended to continue for more than twelve months. It can be deducted in computing a company's trading profits, taxable under Schedule D Case I, provided it is incurred wholly and exclusively for the purposes of the trade. It may alternatively be deducted from the company's miscellaneous profits taxable under Schedule D Case VI, if it is a proper expense of earning those profits (TA 1988 s.9).

Short interest which cannot be deducted in this way can be set off against a company's total profits, provided it is payable in the UK on an advance from a bank, a member of the Stock Exchange, or a discount house carrying on a bona fide business here, and, provided also, that the payment qualifies for relief as a *charge on income* (TA 1988 ss.338(1), (3), 340) (*see further below*).

No relief is available for short interest paid in any other circumstances.

Yearly interest payable in the UK, on an advance from a bank carrying on a bona fide banking business here, can be deducted in computing a company's Case I profits, provided it is paid wholly and exclusively for the purposes of the trade (TA 1988 s.337(3)).

Otherwise, yearly interest can be relieved (if at all) only if it qualifies for relief as a charge on income (TA 1988 ss.337(2)(b), 338(1), (3)(b)).

In general, a payment of interest (short or yearly) will qualify for relief as a charge on income provided that:

(1) it is made under a liability incurred for valuable and sufficient consideration; and

(2) it is ultimately borne by the company making it; and

(3) it is not a distribution of the profits of that company; and

(4) either
    (a) the company exists wholly or mainly for the purposes of carrying on a trade, or
    (b) the interest is paid wholly and exclusively for the purposes of a trade carried on by it, or
    (c) the company is an investment company (*see below*); and

(5) as regards payments of yearly interest to a non-UK resident, the payer company is resident in the UK and either
    (a) the payment is made under deduction of income tax at the basic rate, or
    (b) it is made wholly out of foreign source income, or
    (c) it is interest on a quoted Eurobond (*see further* chapter 7), or
    (d) the company is carrying on a trade and the payment is, broadly, interest payable and paid outside the UK, either for the purposes of the company's trading activities outside the UK or, if paid in a currency other than sterling, for the purposes of the company's trade wherever carried on (TA 1988 ss.338 – 340).

Where a double taxation agreement permits payment without deduction, or at a reduced rate, that is regarded as falling within (5) (a) above.

6.1.2 *Payment of Interest*

Short interest is payable gross. Yearly interest is normally payable under deduction of income tax at the basic rate (TA 1988 s.349(2)). Yearly interest may, however, be paid gross in a number of circumstances, notably where:

(a) it is paid in the UK on an advance from a bank carrying on a bona fide banking business here (TA 1988 s.349(3)(a)); or

(b) it is paid to a non-UK resident and the relevant double taxation agreement authorises payment without deduction (payment gross in these circumstances must be sanctioned by the Inspector of Foreign Dividends); or

(c) it is paid under a foreign source obligation and is therefore not taxable under Schedule D Case III in the hands of the recipient (TA 1988 s.349(2)); or

(d) it is paid between companies in the same group, under an election to that effect made jointly by the payer and payee (TA 1988 s.247(4)); or

(e) it is paid in a fiduciary or representative capacity (TA 1988 s.349(2)(a)); or

(f) it is paid *by* a bank in the ordinary course of its business (TA 1988 s.349(3)(b)).

6.2   Incidental Costs of Obtaining Loan Finance

The incidental costs of obtaining loan finance can be deducted as a trading expense, or as a management expense of an investment company, provided the loan or loan stock is not convertible into shares within three years, and provided also that the interest payable on the loan is deductible for tax purposes, whether as an expense or as a charge on income (TA 1988 s.77). Where the loan or loan stock is convertible within three years, the incidental costs of obtaining it are deductible to the extent that the conversion rights remain unexercised at the end of that period (TA 1988 s.77(3)).

The costs that can be relieved in this way include: professional fees, underwriting commissions, brokerage, introduction and negotiation fees, commitment fees for loan facilities, commission for guaranteeing a loan, advertising, printing, postage and other similar costs.

The cost of insuring against adverse exchange rate movements is specifically excluded (TA 1988 s.77(7)(a)).

6.3   Annual Payments

Certain payments that are interest in economic substance, and are referred to elsewhere in this book, are not interest in law, because generally there is no underlying debtor/creditor relationship between the parties. Nevertheless, they may be relieved as *annual payments*.

Broadly, an annual payment is a payment which is:

(a) of an income nature; and

(b) payable under a legal obligation; and

(c) recurrent, or capable of recurring; and

(d) pure income profit in the hands of the recipient.

Such a payment must be made under deduction of income tax at the basic rate unless:

(a) it arises from land and so is taxable under Schedule A; or

(b) it is paid under a foreign source obligation and so is not chargeable under Schedule D Case III in the hands of the recipient; or

(c) it is paid to a non-UK resident and the relevant double taxation agreement authorises payment without deduction. As before, the sanction of the Inspector of Foreign Dividends is required before payments are made gross (TA 1988 ss.348 – 350).

An annual payment may be relieved as a charge on income of the payer provided:

(a) it is not charged to capital; and

(b) it is ultimately borne by the company making it; and

(c) it is made under a liability incurred for valuable and sufficient consideration (TA 1988 s.338(1), (3)(b), (5)).

6.4   Investment and other Non-trading Companies

An *investment company* is one whose business consists, wholly or mainly, in the making of investments and whose income is principally derived from those investments. An investment company can deduct certain *management expenses* in computing its taxable profits. It should be noted, however, that the relief is restricted, broadly, to the expenses of managing the company rather than those of managing its investments (TA 1988 s.75).

An investment company can also obtain relief for its charges on income, as described above. Thus, short interest paid by such a company will normally be relieved only if paid in the UK on an advance from a bank, a member of the Stock Exchange or a discount house carrying on business here.

A company which is neither a trading nor an investment company can obtain relief for annual payments, but *not* for interest or charges on income. Therefore, interest paid by such a company will go unrelieved.

[7]

QUOTED EUROBONDS

Interest on quoted Eurobonds, that is, on bearer securities issued by a company and quoted on a recognised stock exchange in the UK or overseas, is payable without deduction of tax provided either:

(a) the payment of interest is made by or through an overseas paying agent; or

(b) the payment is made by the company itself or by or through a UK paying agent, and

   (i) it is shown that the person owning the bonds and entitled to the interest is not resident in the UK, or

   (ii) the bond is held in a recognised clearing system, designated as such in an order made by the Inland Revenue (e.g. Cedel and Euro-Clear) (TA 1988 s.124 and SP8/84).

Where payment is made through a subsidiary paying agent, who is put in funds by a principal paying agent, it is the location of the subsidiary agent which will determine whether or not payment can be made gross. Where it cannot, income tax at the basic rate must be deducted from the payment and accounted for to the Inland Revenue in the usual way.

Eurobond interest paid gross under these provisions can be relieved as a charge on income of the paying company, in the same way as annual interest paid under deduction of tax.

Interest received by an investor in Eurobonds is chargeable under Schedule D Case III, tax normally being recovered by direct assessment on the recipient. Where, however, a banker or other person in the UK obtains payment of Eurobond interest abroad (and so gross), or realises such interest coupons for the benefit of a UK resident, income tax at the basic rate will be deductible from the onward payment by that collecting agent.

On the other hand, no attempt will be made to recover tax on Eurobond interest properly paid gross to a non-UK resident.

A Eurobond quoted on a recognised exchange in the UK, denominated in sterling with no provision for conversion into, or redemption in, any other currency, and issued on normal commercial terms, will also be a qualifying corporate bond within TA 1984 s.64. It will therefore be free of capital gains tax on any intermediate disposal. Such disposal may, however, attract a charge to tax under the accrued income scheme (TA 1988 ss.710 – 728).

[8]

DEEP DISCOUNT
SECURITIES

8.1 Definition

A deep discount security is one that carries a lower rate of interest than comparable securities issued at a price equal to redemption value, but which is issued at a discount to par, such that its overall yield to maturity represents a market rate of interest.

A zero coupon bond is a deep discount security that carries no interest. The whole of its yield to maturity is comprised in the discount at which it is issued.

8.2 Basis of Taxation

As a general rule, a discount receivable, other than in a financial trade, will be charged to tax under Schedule D Case III when received. A discount payable otherwise than in a financial trade may be deducted in computing the trading profits of the paying company, provided it is paid wholly and exclusively for the purposes of the relevant trade and in respect of short-term finance. Otherwise, a discount payable may be relieved (if at all) as a charge on income, but only if paid on a bill of exchange by a trading or investment company (*see* TA 1988 s.78).

When the Treasury first authorised the issue of sterling deep discount securities in 1982, this was on the expectation that they would follow the US model and provide for the daily accrual of 'discount' in the event of early redemption. The Inland Revenue indeed stated that they regarded the discount on such securities as representing a reward for the use of money, and so as interest. This view is consistent with the finding in *Willingale* v. *International Commercial Bank Ltd* [1978] STC 35. However, this case also held that whilst interest accrues from day to day, or at other fixed intervals, discount does not.

Accordingly, under general law, the discount on a deep discount security will be charged to tax as rolled-up interest in the hands of the recipient at redemption, regardless of the price the purchaser paid for the security. Similarly, the whole of the discount may be set off against the paying company's profits for the accounting period in which the security is redeemed.

Subject, in the case of interest bearing securities, to the possible application of the accrued income scheme, intermediate sales of deep discount securities are liable only to capital gains tax. Such intermediate sales and tax effects are of no interest to the issuing company. Furthermore, if the redemption proceeds of the security, less the amount of discount taxed as the income of its holder at redemption, is less than his acquisition cost, he may be entitled to a capital loss at that time.

The above treatment continues to apply to deep discount securities that are not subject to the special provisions originally introduced in the Finance Act 1984 (now in TA 1988 s.57 and Schedule 4). These are described below.

8.3 TA 1988 Schedule 4

Section 57 and Schedule 4 TA 1988 provide for the tax treatment of certain deep discount, including zero coupon, securities issued after 13 March 1984.

The securities concerned are, broadly, redeemable securities issued by a company at a discount to par of more than 0.5 per cent for each complete year of their life or more than 15 per cent overall, and which:

(a) do not comprise shares of the issuing company; and

(b) are not redeemable at an amount which is index-linked; and

(c) are not issued by way of a bonus issue to existing shareholders.

Where these conditions are satisfied, then for the issuer the discount at which the stock is issued is treated as interest arising on a compound yield basis over the period to redemption.

In general, the issuing company can obtain relief for that 'interest' on an accruals basis, as if it were a charge on income, provided that:

(a) the cost of paying the discount is ultimately borne by the company; and

(b) the 'interest' is not otherwise deductible in computing the company's profits; and

(c) either

   (i) the company exists wholly or mainly for the purpose of carrying on a trade, or

   (ii) the security was issued exclusively for the purposes of a trade carried on by the company, or

   (iii) the company is an investment company; and

(d) no part of the redemption proceeds of the security will be treated as a distribution of the company.

The investor in such deep discount securities is normally taxed on the 'interest' arising over his period of ownership of the securities, but only on their redemption or disposal. The death of an individual investor constitutes a disposal. Where the difference between the investor's purchase cost and his disposal proceeds is greater or less than the accrued income, that excess or shortfall is treated as a capital gain or loss.

It will be noted that this statutory treatment is deliberately asymmetrical between lender and borrower. Assuming tax rates are constant, it represents a cash flow disadvantage to the Revenue. If rates fall, it represents a real loss of tax. For this reason certain anti-abuse measures were introduced at the same time.

Where a deep discount security is held by a company which is a member of the same group as the issuing company, or is otherwise under common control, relief for the interest attributable to that company's period of ownership is available to the issuing company only in the accounting period in which the security is redeemed. A similar restriction applies where the stock is issued by a close company and is held by a participator in that company or by someone closely associated with him.

Finally, in this context, it should be noted that:

(a) the incidental costs of issuing deep discount securities are specifically brought within the relief for incidental costs of loan finance in TA 1988 s.77 (*see* section 6.2);

(b) any interest actually payable in respect of such a security will be relieved and taxed according to the normal rules for the taxation of interest paid and received (including the accrued income scheme);

(c) there is no requirement to deduct tax from the discount when it is 'paid' on the redemption of the security.

8.4   Coupon Stripping

Following the introduction of the provisions described above, it became possible to defer tax by investing in a series of zero coupon bonds, the proceeds of the investment being onward invested by the issuing company in gilts. Interest received by that company would be matched by 'interest' accruing on the zero coupon bonds, eliminating any charge to tax. The investor's annual return would mostly comprise the redemption proceeds of one of the bonds, substantially free of tax.

Where deep discount securities are issued in these circumstances on or after 19 March 1985, the investor will be charged to tax on his 'interest' as it accrues, rather than on receipt. These provisions will also apply where the company issuing the deep discount securities does not invest directly in gilts but in UK corporate bonds issued by another company.

A 'UK corporate bond' is any bond issued by a company resident in the UK on normal commercial terms and which is denominated in sterling and carries no rights of conversion into, or redemption in, any other currency (TA 1988 Schedule 4 para 2(8)).

8.5 Financial Traders

As mentioned above, it was held in *Willingale* v. *International Commercial Bank Ltd* [1978] STC 75 that discounts received did not accrue from day to day, or for any other fixed periods, and could not therefore be taxed until received. This applied even though they were brought into the accounts on an accruals basis.

The discounts received by the bank were on medium-term bills of exchange with a life of between one and ten years. The Revenue was dissatisfied with the judgement and has sought to restrict its application to its own facts. It continues, therefore, to accept computations from banks and other financial traders which bring in discounts on short-term paper on the normal accountancy accruals basis. In practice, it will accept adjustment to the statutory accounts figures only where the auditors confirm that they would have given an unqualified report if the accounts had excluded accrued discounts *and* the bills for which the 'receipts basis' is claimed were originally issued with a life of at least twelve months.

Whilst the legal validity of this distinction between discounts on short- and medium-term paper must be doubted, it is certainly convenient and practical in most circumstances for the tax treatment of such transactions to follow the accounts.

[9]

STERLING COMMERCIAL PAPER

9.1 Definition

Sterling commercial paper (SCP) comprises negotiable short-term unsecured promissory notes denominated in sterling and payable to the bearer. SCP can carry interest, but normally it is issued with a zero coupon and at a discount to face value; in any event, it is always dealt in on the basis of its yield to maturity.

The issue of SCP is hedged around with many complex restrictions. Broadly:

- the issuing company, or its 100 per cent parent, must have ordinary or preference shares listed on the Stock Exchange; and

- the issuing company, or its 100 per cent parent, must have net assets of not less than £50 m; and

- the paper itself must have a minimum face value of £500,000; and

- it must have a term of not less than seven days but not more than one year; and

- it must be guaranteed either by the 100 per cent parent or by a recognised bank or licensed deposit taker (BA 1979 (Exempt Transactions) Regs. 1986, reg. 15).

9.2 Basis of Taxation

Given that SCP must, by definition, have a life of less than one year, it is unlikely to be issued at a discount to par of more than 15 per cent. It is also difficult to see how it can be at a discount of 0.5 per cent 'for each complete year' of its life.

Nevertheless, the Inland Revenue takes the view that SCP is a deep discount security capable of falling within the provisions of TA 1988 s.57 and Schedule 4 (*see also* chapter 8).

The Revenue's argument appears to be that SCP with a life of, say, six months has a life of one half of a complete year and will therefore fall within the 1984 regime if it is issued at a discount of more than half of 0.5 per cent or 0.25 per cent to par.

The Revenue also regards SCP as being a form of certificate of deposit for the purposes of TA 1988 s.56. A certificate of deposit is a document acknowledging that money, in any currency, has been deposited with the issuer or some other person. Such a document recognises an obligation to pay a stated amount to bearer or to order, with or without interest. It is a document by the delivery of which, with or without endorsement, the right to receive that stated amount, with or without interest, is transferable (FA 1968 s.55(3)).

A company issuing SCP will obtain relief for the discount paid on it either as a deduction in computing its trading profits, if the funds are raised wholly and exclusively for the purposes of the relevant trade, or, provided the conditions in TA 1988 Schedule 4 are satisfied, under the deep discount security legislation described in chapter 8. In either case, relief will be given on an accruals basis and the discount, when paid, will be without deduction of tax.

Any interest payable on SCP will be short interest. If the discount on SCP is deductible in computing trading profits, so also will be the interest. If this was not the case, no relief would be due since the interest would not be payable on an advance from a UK bank, discount house or member of the Stock Exchange. It is because the issuing companies are often holding companies of large groups, and therefore not necessarily trading companies in their own right, that it is normal for all the interest to be in the form of discount to maturity. It is therefore convenient that the Revenue regards them as falling under the deep discount security provisions.

The incidental costs of making the issue will be relieved under Schedule D Case I if the discount is relieved under Case

I, and TA 1988 s.77 if the discount is relieved under the deep discount legislation, but not otherwise.

An investor in SCP who is assessable under Schedule D Case I on dealings in securities will bring both the discount and any interest received into his Case I computations, in the usual way.

Other investors, in the Revenue's view, will be taxed under TA 1988 s.56. This implies that any gain on the disposal or maturity of the SCP, including the discount, will be taxed under Case III.

[10]

FINANCIAL FUTURES

10.1 Background

A financial futures contract is a standardised agreement to buy or sell a fixed amount of a specified financial instrument at a predetermined future date. They are generally traded on an official exchange – for example, the London International Financial Futures Exchange (LIFFE).

Such contracts normally relate to one of the following:

(a) future interest rates on a specified instrument;

(b) future exchange rates between specified currencies;

(c) future levels of a specified recognised stock index;

(d) future values of a specified security.

Futures contracts could run to delivery but in practice will be 'closed out' before settlement by the acquisition of an equal and opposite contract. The difference between the two contract prices will be settled in cash.

Financial futures can either be traded for profit or used to hedge other transactions, effectively locking the user into the market's projected future rate, level or value.

10.2 Basis of Taxation – Trading Transactions

Where a bank, or other financial trader, deals in financial futures, the profits or losses will form part of its Schedule D Case I computation. A company which deals in futures for profit may also be taxed on its dealing profits and losses under Schedule D Case I, if those dealings amount to the

45

carrying on of a trade. The issues are the same as for options and have already been dealt with in chapter 4.

Further, a company other than a financial trader which deals in futures wholly to hedge transactions on revenue account may also bring its profits or losses on the hedge into the computation of taxable profits of the underlying trade (*see* SP4/88 para. 11).

Where dealings in futures do fall to be taxed under Schedule D Case I, the profit or loss should, as a general rule, be computed on a realisation basis. This is because neither profit nor loss should be anticipated for tax purposes. Where, however, contracts which are open at the end of the accounting period are brought into account at their 'marked to market' value, the Revenue will in practice accept the same approach for tax purposes, provided both profit- and loss-making contracts are marked to market and provided also that the same treatment is applied consistently from year to year.

10.3 Basis of Taxation – Non-trading Transactions

Prior to 6 April 1985, profits and losses arising from transactions in financial futures not forming part of a trade were normally taxed as income profits and losses under Schedule D Case VI, even when used to hedge capital transactions.

Since that date, such profits and losses have been taxed as capital gains and losses, provided they have arisen from transactions on LIFFE or on any other futures exchange in the UK or elsewhere which is recognised by the Inland Revenue. Since 2 July 1986, futures in gilts and qualifying corporate bonds have been exempt from capital gains tax (FA 1986 s.59).

For capital gains tax purposes, the closing out of one futures contract by the acquisition of a reciprocal contract constitutes the disposal of an asset (the outstanding obligations under the original contract) on which a chargeable gain or allowable loss may arise. Accordingly, any money or money's worth received by the taxpayer on that event is treated as consideration for the disposal and any money or money's worth paid away by him as incidental costs of making the disposal (FA 1985 s.72(3)).

Where a financial futures contract runs to delivery, and thereupon requires cash settlement, that too is treated as a disposal of the obligations under the contract and sums paid or received by the taxpayer are treated as costs or proceeds of that disposal (FA 1985 s.72(4)).

10.4 Statement of Practice SP4/88

In its Statement of Practice SP4/88, published on 25 July 1988, the Inland Revenue confirmed that where a transaction in financial futures or options is clearly related to an underlying transaction, asset or portfolio, the tax treatment of the futures or option contract will follow that of the underlying transaction, asset or portfolio. Such a relationship is regarded as existing where the future or option is used as a hedge to reduce the risk attaching to the underlying transaction, asset or portfolio.

A transaction will be treated as a hedge for these purposes if:

(a) it is economically appropriate to the reduction in risk of the underlying transaction, asset or portfolio; and

(b) the price fluctuations of the options or futures are directly and demonstrably related to the fluctuations in value or composition of the underlying transaction, asset or portfolio, at the time the hedge is initiated.

This treatment applies to all futures and options, whether traded on an exchange or otherwise.

[11]
INTEREST RATE SWAPS

11.1   Analysis of Transaction

The interest rate swap can reduce finance costs. The swap exploits different interest rates across markets, across borrowers and between types of borrowing, such as between fixed and floating rates. Swap transactions can become complex. There may be a number of counterparties operating across as many tax jurisdictions.

An example of a simple interest rate swap transaction is set out below. It has two counterparties and is in only one currency. It should be borne in mind that a bank will stand between the companies in practice. This is to bear the credit risk and simplify the tax treatment of·the swap payments. In return, the bank will take a small return on the deal. The bank has not been included in the example to keep it simple.

Example

	Rate p.a.
Company X is a high-quality credit and can borrow fixed rate for 5 years at:	14%
Or it can borrow at a floating rate of LIBOR (say 12 per cent) plus $\frac{3}{8}$ per cent:	$12\frac{3}{8}\%$
Company Y is a poorer credit and if it could borrow at a fixed rate it would be at:	16%
Or it can borrow at a variable rate of LIBOR plus 1 per cent:	13%

LIBOR is a variable market rate, London Inter Bank Offered Rate. It is the rate at which on any day prime London banks will lend funds to each other.

Thus there is 2 per cent differential in the market between the fixed rates these borrowers can command but only a $\frac{5}{8}$ per cent difference between the variable rates.

Assume that Company X requires floating rate debt whereas Company Y requires fixed rate debt.

X borrows fixed rate. Y borrows variable rate. They also enter into a swap agreement. Under this agreement a payment of $2\frac{5}{8}$ per cent (but linked to LIBOR) will be made from Y to X. If LIBOR rises by more than $2\frac{5}{8}$ per cent, the payment will go from X to Y.

	With LIBOR at 12%	With LIBOR at 14%
Company X		
X borrows fixed at	14	14
Y pays X	$(2\frac{5}{8})$	$(\frac{5}{8})$
X total cost variable	$11\frac{3}{8}$	$13\frac{3}{8}$
Compared with LIBOR based rate	$12\frac{3}{8}$	$14\frac{3}{8}$
Saving	1	1
Company Y		
Y borrows variable at (LIBOR + 1)	13	15
Y pays A	$2\frac{5}{8}$	$\frac{5}{8}$
Y total cost fixed	$15\frac{5}{8}$	$15\frac{5}{8}$
Compared with fixed rate	16	16
Saving	$\frac{3}{8}$	$\frac{3}{8}$
Total savings X & Y	$1\frac{3}{8}$	$1\frac{3}{8}$

11.2   Treatment of Compensatory Payments

The swap compensatory payments made between the parties are payments computed in accordance with the agreement. They are normally related to movements in a market rate such as LIBOR. Because they are not actually payments of interest, they cannot be treated as interest for tax purposes. Periodic payments will only qualify as interest if they represent 'payment by time for the use of money' (*Bennett* v. *Ogston* [1930] 15 TC 374) and are paid in respect of a debt (*Re Euro Hotel* [*Belgravia*] *Ltd* [1975] 51 TC 293).

However, since the periodic compensatory payments are clearly contractual, may prove recurrent and are of an income nature, they will be annual payments (*CIR* v. *Whitworth Park Coal Co. Ltd* [1959] 38 TC 531).

There are two considerations that arise: firstly, as to whether a UK resident counterparty will have to deduct 25 per cent (current) basic rate withholding tax from compensatory payments; and, secondly, how will the compensatory payments obtain tax relief?

11.2.1 Withholding Tax

The position depends on the nature of the counterparty and whether it is acting as principal or agent. The general legal position is that withholding tax must be deducted from annual payments if they represent pure income profit in the hands of the recipient. This means that they are income against which expenses cannot be offset (*Re Hanbury* [1939] 38 TC 588 and *CIR* v. *Campbell* [1968] 45 TC 427).

It follows therefore that

(a) payments made between counterparties not engaged in a financial trade are subject to withholding tax;

(b) payments to a financial trader, acting as principal, are not pure profit income and can be made without such deduction; and

(c) payments by a financial trader, acting as principal, are subject to withholding tax, unless they originate outside the UK or they flow from the UK to overseas and the recipient can obtain withholding tax exemption under a double tax treaty. Article 21, the 'other income' article, of the OECD model treaty provides such exemption.

The Revenue's practice, though, is to allow swap payments by recognised banks (*not* all financial traders) acting as principal, to be made free of withholding tax.

11.2.2 *Tax Relief*

(a) *Legal position*

As swap compensatory payments are annual payments, a deduction cannot be obtained as a trading expense (TA 1988 s.74(m)), but periodic payments will qualify as a charge on income (TA 1988 s.338(3)). Under the latter section, a tax deduction is obtainable for annual payments made to a UK resident, even if withholding tax has not been applied.

If the payment is made to a non-resident, withholding tax must be deducted in order for the annual payment to qualify as a charge on income, unless exemption is available under an applicable double tax treaty or the payment is made out of foreign income chargeable under Schedule D Case IV or Case V.

(b) *Revenue practice*

Commonly the Revenue adopts a more liberal approach for payments made by UK trading companies. Provided the payment is made to a recognised UK bank, it will be allowed as a trading expense deductible on the accruals basis. This approach may not necessarily be accepted in the case of long-term swaps.

This is because the swaps could be regarded as being on capital account and TA 1988 s.74(g) would prohibit relief as a trading expense. In this case, relief would remain available on a paid basis as a charge on income.

It follows that it is normally preferable to have a bank act as a principal on both sides of the swap transaction, to minimise tax problems.

11.3   Fees

The fees paid to banks and other intermediaries for setting up swap transactions will be trading income of the banks and will be taxed accordingly. Prior to the Finance Act 1980, such fees paid by companies (if not banks) were not normally deductible as a trading expense if they related to the costs of raising finance of a capital nature. Also, in relation to investment companies, such fees were not deductible as management expenses. TA 1988 s.77 now allows the deduction of certain expenses as part of the incidental costs of obtaining loan finance.

The problem with swap arrangement fees is that the costs of setting up swap transactions are not at the moment regarded as such payments, even though they are usually part of a financing programme. So, as the law and practice presently stand, a tax deduction is not usually available in the UK. It may, therefore, become necessary to include the set-up fees in the compensatory payments to the bank to obtain relief.

[12]

FORWARD RATE AGREEMENTS (FRAs)

12.1 Background

An FRA is an interest rate management technique. It is a contract, generally with a bank, that provides for compensatory payments to be made, calculated according to a notional amount of principal at a fixed interest rate for a fixed future period. If, at the beginning of the relevant future period, prevailing interest rates have increased beyond the agreed interest rate for a borrowing, the seller of the FRA will compensate the purchaser for the excess. If, however, interest rates fall below the agreed rate, the purchaser will compensate the seller for the shortfall.

For example, on 1 January a company knows that it will need to borrow £20 m for six months from 1 July. It wishes to protect itself against any rise in interest rates between 1 January and 1 July, beyond the prevailing level of 13 per cent. It therefore purchases an FRA from a bank for a period of six months commencing on 1 July, based on a notional principal of £20 m and an agreed interest rate of 13 per cent.

On 1 July, the company will borrow the £20 m required in the cash market. It will not necessarily borrow from the seller of the FRA because the FRA is entirely independent of the underlying debt. If the prevailing interest rate is then 14 per cent per annum, the seller of the FRA will pay the company an amount equal to the excess interest (1 per cent per annum) on the notional FRA principal (£20 m) for the agreed period (six months); in this case a compensatory payment of the present value of £100,000.

If on the other hand, the six-month rate prevailing on 1 July

53

is only 12 per cent, the company will have to pay compensation to the seller of the FRA of the present value of £100,000.

12.2 Basis of Taxation

Since there is no indebtedness between the parties to an FRA, compensatory payments made under it, although computed by reference to interest rates, are not themselves interest. Neither, since FRAs are generally short-term agreements, are they annual payments for the purposes of TA 1988 s.338. This section gives relief for such payments as charges on income.

Banks and other financial institutions will normally treat FRA compensatory payments as trading expenses and compensatory receipts as trading receipts, for tax purposes. This is because they will either have sold the agreement in the course of their trade, or used the FRA as a tool of interest rate risk management. This is, of course, an inherent part of their trade.

Similarly, non-financial traders will generally be able to treat FRA compensatory payments and receipts as trading items, where the FRA is used to hedge the cost of circulating capital. Otherwise, their compensatory receipts will be taxed under Schedule D Case VI or Case V if they have a foreign source. However, any compensatory payments made by them will go unrelieved. Although from the company's point of view, payment under an FRA is a cost of the related borrowing, it cannot be relieved as an incidental cost of obtaining loan finance under TA 1988 s.77.

Investment companies will also be taxed on their FRA compensatory receipts under Schedule D Case V or VI, but will obtain no relief for payments made by them; such payments are not expenses of management within TA 1988 s.75.

Where the FRA is not of an income nature, for example if it is used to hedge a single capital transaction, it will itself be regarded as a capital item and the normal capital gains tax rules will apply.

$[13]$
INTEREST RATE GUARANTEES (IRGs)

13.1 Background

An IRG enables the treasurer to hedge against an unfavourable movement in interest rates but without fixing any particular rate, should rates stay the same or move in his favour. In substance, such a guarantee is an interest rate option.

For example, in consideration of a premium received, a bank guarantees that a future borrowing rate will not exceed 13 per cent. If the rate does exceed 13 per cent at the guarantee date, the bank pays the customer the present value of the difference. If the rate is below this at the guarantee date, the customer abandons the guarantee and borrows at the lower rate. Hence the contract is an interest rate option. Sometimes these contracts are called interest rate caps if they are for long periods.

Equally, a treasurer may purchase a guarantee that interest rates will not fall below a set level (a 'floor' agreement) or, by combining cap and floor agreements, that interest rates will stay within a predetermined band. Such a combination of options is called a 'collar'.

As with swaps and FRAs, IRGs are quite independent of the financial arrangements to which they relate. They need not be purchased from bankers involved with those arrangements.

13.2 Basis of Taxation

The UK tax treatment of the premium for an interest rate guarantee and any profit on exercise is similar to that for forward rate agreements (*see* section 12.2).

Where the company concerned is a bank or other financial institution, both payments will be of a trading nature and will be included as income or expense in the Schedule D Case I computation. For other companies, the tax treatment will depend on the specific circumstances and the reasons for the transaction. There are circumstances where the payments will be accepted as trading items. Thus, if an IRG is used to hedge a particular capital transaction, asset or portfolio, the tax treatment of the IRG will follow that of the transaction, asset or portfolio concerned. If, on the other hand, the IRG were used to protect the company against adverse interest rate movements pending a bond issue, or as part of a change in its investment strategy, the IRG will be taxed as a capital transaction, even though it is not a hedging transaction. Where, however, the company uses IRGs incidentally to its trading activities, profits or losses on the IRGs will form part of its Schedule D Case I profits or losses (*see* Inland Revenue Statement of Practice SP4/88, (1988) STI 590).

Again, as with FRA payments, premiums paid do not rank as management expenses of investment companies under TA 1988 s.75. Such companies will not, therefore, obtain any deduction for IRG premiums.

Withholding tax will not be deductible from the payments under the provisions of TA 1988 ss.349 and 350, since the payments are neither interest nor annual payments.

IRGs are normally 'over-the-counter' agreements made between a bank and its customer, tailormade to the customer's needs. If the customer does not require such a bespoke transaction, it may purchase a traded option on an interest rate financial future. In this case, the tax treatment will be the same as for other traded options. This is set out in detail in chapter 4.

INDEX

Accountancy practice (SSAP 20) 8–9, 12
Annual payments 33; forward rate
  agreements (FRAs) 54

Badges of trade 20
Banks 4, 54, 56
Bearer securities *see* Quoted Eurobonds
Borrowings, foreign currency 3; *see also*
  Interest; Loan finance

Call options 22
Capital 3, 9–10
Capital allowances 15–16
Capital gains: currency swaps 29;
  financial futures 46–7; foreign exchange
  gains and losses 16–18; indexation
  allowances 16; traded options 21–2
Certainty 2
Chicago Futures Exchange 19
Collar 55
Companies, tax status of 3–4; *see also*
  Groups of companies *and individual*
  forms, e.g. Investment companies
Compensatory payments forward rate
  agreements (FRAs) 54; interest rate
  swaps 49–51
Corporate bonds, UK 40
Corporation tax: currency swaps 29
Costs: interest rate swaps fees 51–2; loan
  finance 32–3; sterling commercial
  paper 43–4
Coupon stripping 40
Currency swaps 11, 25–9; capital
  gains 29; corporation tax 29; gains
  and losses 28–9; interest differential
  payments 27; set-up costs 27–8; tax
  implications 27–9; transactions 25–7

Deep discount securities 37–41
Double taxation agreement 31

Eurobonds *see* Quoted Eurobonds
Exchange gains and losses *see* Foreign
  exchange gains and losses

Financial futures 23; background 45;
  capital gains tax 46–7; closed out
  contracts 45; currency

transactions 15; marked to market 46;
  non-trading transactions 46–7;
  SP4/88 47; taxation basis 45–6;
  trading transactions 45–6
Financial options *see* Options
Foreign currency borrowings 3;
  options 19–20
Foreign exchange gains and losses 5–18;
  accountancy practice 8–9; capital
  allowances 15–16; capital
  gains 16–18; groups of companies 3;
  hedging transactions 5, 12;
  matching 9–10; non-monetary
  assets 8–9; non-trading
  companies 14–15; on translation 6;
  overseas branches and trades 12–13;
  Pattison v. *Marine Midland Ltd* 6–8;
  realisation basis 13;
  roundabouts 13–14; SP1/87 7–8,
  9–10, 13, 14, 28–9; swaps 11, 28–9;
  unmatched positions 10–11
Forward rate agreements (FRAs) 53–4;
  annual payments 54; compensatory
  payments 54; taxation basis 54
Futures *see* Financial futures

Groups of companies 2–3

Hedging 24; currency options 19–20;
  exchange gains and losses 12

Insurance 33
Interest 4; annual payments 33;
  deductibility 30–2; deep discount
  securities 37–41; differential
  payments 27; forward rate agreements
  (FRAs) 54; payment of 31–2; relief
  for 30–1; short 30, 31; sterling
  commercial paper and 43; yearly 30,
  31–2; *see also* Interest rate guarantees
  (IRGs); Interest rate swaps
Interest rate guarantees (IRGs) 55–6;
  caps 55; collar 55; floor
  agreement 55; over-the-counter
  agreements 56; taxation basis 55–6;
  withholding tax 56

Interest rate swaps 48–52; analysis of transaction 48–9; compensatory payments 49–51; fees 51–2; tax relief 51; withholding tax 50–1
Investment companies 4, 56; forward rate agreements (FRAs) 54; management expenses 34

Land, sale of foreign 5
LIFFE *see* London International Financial Futures Exchange (LIFFE)
Loan finance 30–4; annual payments 33; incidental costs of 32–3; interest deductibility 30–2; investment companies 34; relief for interest paid 30–1; *see also* Borrowings
London Inter Bank Offered Rate (LIBOR) 48, 49
London International Financial Futures Exchange (LIFFE) 19, 45, 46
London Stock Exchange 19

Matching 9–10; unmatched positions 10–11

Non-trading transactions: financial futures 46–7; foreign exchange gains and losses 14–15; options 21–2

Options: background 19–24; call options 22; capital gains 21–2; exchange traded 19; foreign currency 19–20; hedging 24; non-trading transactions 21–2; over-the-counter 19, 23–4; put options 22; trading transactions 20–1: *see also* Financial futures
Over-the-counter options 23–4; in financial futures 23

Pattison v. *Marine Midland Ltd* 6–8

Philadelphia Stock Exchange 19
Promissory notes *see* Sterling commercial paper
Put options 22

Quoted Eurobonds 35–6; clearing systems 35; coupon stripping 40; death of investor 39; definition 37; financial traders 41; TA 1988 Schedule 4 38–40; taxation basis 37–8

Ramsay doctrine 14
Realisation basis foreign exchange gains and losses 13; futures 46; trading options 21
Revenue 3, 9–10
Roundabouts 13–14

Short interest 30, 31
SSAPs *see* Accountancy practice
Statements of Practice: SP1/87 7–8, 9–10, 13, 14, 28–9; SP4/88 47
Sterling commercial paper: certificate of deposit 43; costs 43–4; definition 42; interest payable 43; taxation basis 42–4
Subsidiaries 2
Swaps, currency *see* Currency swaps

Traders 20, 41, 46
Trading transactions financial futures 45–6; options 20–1

UK corporate bond 40
Unmatched positions 10–11

Withholding tax 50–1; interest rate guarantees (IRGs) 56

Yearly interest 30, 31–2

Zero coupon bonds 37, 38